Called To Be Trees Of Righteousness

Nature Commends Us To God's Supernatural

I0429370

"The Spirit of the Lord God is upon me ... to give unto them beauty for ashes, the oil of joy for mourning, the garment of praise for the spirit of heaviness; that they might be called trees of righteousness the planting of the Lord, that he might be glorified."

Isaiah 61:1-3 cf. Isaiah 55:12-13b

L. Phillip Schmidt
Esther Grace Schmidt

Graphic Credits
 Front Cover: CreateSpace. Back Cover: Photograph – Courtesy of Olan Mills Portrait Studios. Charts: Covenant Of Sovereign Grace Ministry. Clip Art: RaisngOurKids.com. 11. Free Public Domain. 1, 3a, 15, 27, 29, 47. ChristiansUnite.com. 2b, 3b, 18, 20, 22, 26a, 31, 32, 46. WPclipart.com. 2a, 6, 8, 10, 12, 13, 15, 16, 17, 24, 26b, 34, 35, 36, 37, 54.

Publisher: Covenant Of Sovereign Grace Ministry
Forth Edition: January 2019
Copyright © 2016, 2017, 2018, 2019 L. Phillip Schmidt and Esther Grace Schmidt

ISBN-13: 978-1532736940   ISBN-10: 1532736940

This Book Is Dedicated

To

God The Father
God The Son
God The Holy Spirit

For

Revealing Themselves To Us In
All They Have Made

And

For The Everlasting Life Given
To Those Who Faithfully Believe

Contents

Introduction

WHILE upon this earth, Jesus often turned the attention of His listeners towards nature to illustrate His Kingdom by using various parables, metaphors, and symbolic language in an endeavor to help them understand Spiritual Truths of the Supernatural of both seen and Unseen all about them.

Humankind has only to look around them and know that they themselves were not made by chance; because the effective causation of the Supernatural brought into existence that never was – unto, into, and onto the existence of all things – including our human existence.

The purpose of this book is to elaborate on the Spiritual Lessons to be learned as we consider some of the natural instincts and intuitive acclivities, proclivities and declivities of the laws of nature which God in His Wisdom has created, especially for us to learn of Him by, and NOT to worship the creation – as the world may – but rather the Creator!

It seems that *everyone has a certain sense of right and wrong* which is aptly described by the Apostle Paul writing to the Believers in Rome. "When Gentiles who have not the [divine] Law *do instinctively what the Law requires*, they are a law to themselves, since they do not have the Law. *They show that the essential requirements of the Law are written in their hearts and are operating there*, with which their consciences (sense of right and wrong) also bear witness; and their [moral] decisions (their arguments of reason, their condemning or approving thoughts) will accuse or perhaps defend and excuse [them]." Romans 2:14-15 (Amp.) [lps].

"There are *things about God that people cannot see* – his eternal power and all the things that make him God. But since the beginning of the world those things have been easy to understand. *They are made clear by what God has made*. So people have no excuse for the bad things they do." Romans 1:20 (EB) [lps]. "*No one has seen God*, but *Jesus is exactly like him*. Christ ranks higher than all the things that have been made. *Through his power all things were made – things in heaven and on earth, things seen and unseen*, all powers, authorities, lords, and rulers. All things were made through Christ and for Christ. Christ was there before anything was made. And all things continue because of him." Colossians 1:15-17 (EB) [lps]. *"The heavens tell the glory of God.*

And the skies announce what his hands have made. Day after day they tell the story. Night after night they tell it again. They don't make any sound to be heard. But their message goes out through all the world. It goes everywhere on earth. The sky is like a home for the sun. The sun comes out like a bridegroom from his bedroom. It rejoices like an athlete eager to run a race. The sun rises at one end of the sky, and it follows its path to the other end. Nothing hides from its heat. The Lord's teachings are perfect. They give new strength. The Lord's rules can be trusted. They make plain people wise." Psalm 19:1-7 (EB) [lps].

"Before the world began, there was the Word. The Word was with God, and the Word was God. He was with God in the beginning. All things were made through him. Nothing was made without him.... The Word became a man and lived among us. We saw his glory – the glory that belongs to the only Son of the Father. ... The Word was full of grace and truth. From him we all received more and more blessings. ... *No man has ever seen God. But God the only Son is very close to the Father. And the Son has shown us what God is like.*" John 1:1-3, 14, 16-18 (EB) [lps].

The Supernatural Omnipotence Of God

ONE of the most effective illustrations in nature to help us understand the Supernatural Omnipotence of the Three Persons of the Godhead is a tree. The **Roots** being represented of <u>God The Father</u>. The **Trunk** being represented as <u>God The Son</u>. The **Branches** being represented as <u>God The Holy Spirit</u>; with the **leaves/blossoms/fruit** represented as <u>people</u> created after God's Own Image (Genesis 1:26); and ordained marriage so that man and woman, united as one, continue to procreate after their kind.

Even though the word "Trinity" is not found in the Bible, we learn from several Scripture references that the Godhead consists of Three Persons.

The Trinity Revealed At Christ's Baptism

"At that time Jesus came from the town of Nazareth in Galilee to the place where John was. John baptized Jesus in the Jordan River. When **Jesus** was coming up out of the water, he saw heaven open. The **Holy Spirit** came down on him like a dove. A **voice came from heaven and said: 'You are my Son** and I love you. I am very pleased with you.'" Mark 1:9-10 (EB) [lps].

"The Spirit descended dovelike upon Jesus, and the voice from heaven proclaimed the Father's approval of Jesus as his divine Son. That Jesus is God's divine Son is the foundation for all we read about Jesus in the Gospels. Here we see all three members of the **Trinity together – God the Father, God the Son, and God the Holy Spirit**." – *Life Application Bible,* p. 1637 [lps].

Jesus Talks About The Trinity

"Once when he [Jesus] was eating with them [disciples], he [*Jesus*] told them not to leave Jerusalem. He said, 'The **Father** has made you a promise which I told you about before. Wait here to receive this promise. John baptized people with water, but in a few days you will be baptized with the **Holy Spirit**.'" Acts 1:4-5 (EB) [lps].

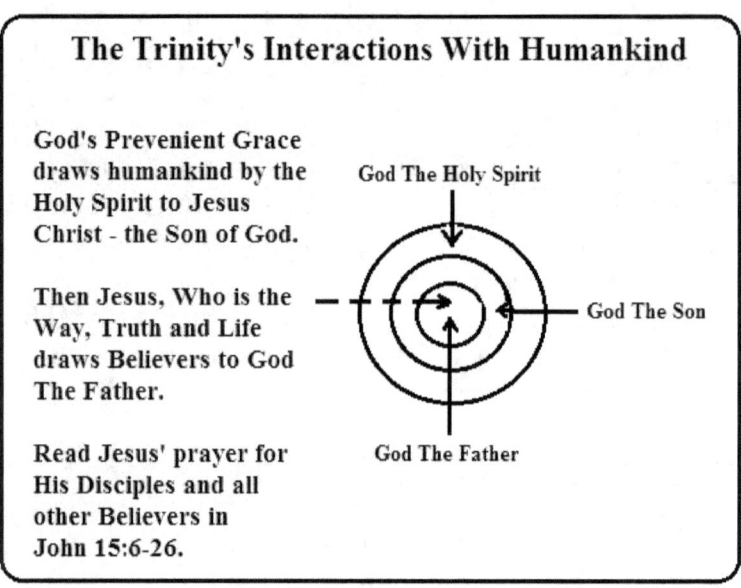

The Trinity's Interactions With Humankind

God's Prevenient Grace draws humankind by the Holy Spirit to Jesus Christ - the Son of God.

Then Jesus, Who is the Way, Truth and Life draws Believers to God The Father.

Read Jesus' prayer for His Disciples and all other Believers in John 15:6-26.

God The Holy Spirit

God The Son

God The Father

"Jesus instructed his disciples to witness to people of all nations about him (Matthew 28:19, 20). But they were told to wait first for the Holy Spirit. *God has important work for you to do for him, but you must do it by the power of the Holy Spirit*. We often like to get on with the job, even if it means running ahead of God. But waiting is sometimes part of God's plan. Are you waiting and listening for God's complete instructions, or are you running ahead of his plans? *We need God's timing and power to be truly effective. ...* We receive the Holy Spirit (are baptized by him) when we receive Jesus Christ. The baptism of the Holy Spirit must be understood in the light of his total work in Christians. (1) The Spirit marks the beginning of the Christian experience We cannot belong to Christ without his Spirit (Romans 8:9); we cannot be united to Christ without his Spirit (1 Corinthians 6:17); we cannot be adopted as his children without his Spirit (Romans 8:14-17; Galatians 4:6, 7); we cannot be in the body of Christ except by baptism in the Spirit (1 Corinthians 12:13). (2) *The Spirit is the power of our new lives.* He begins a lifelong process of change as we become more like Christ (Galatians 3:3, Philippians 1:6). When we receive Christ by faith, we begin an immediate *personal relationship* with God. The Holy Spirit works in us to help us become like Christ. (3) The Spirit unites the Christian community in Christ (Ephesians 2:19-22). *The Holy Spirit can be experienced by all and works through all* (1 Corinthians 12:11; Ephesians 4:4)." – *Life Application Bible,* pp. 1870-1871 [lps].

The Apostle Peter Wrote About The Trinity

"Elect according to the foreknowledge of **God the Father**, through sanctification of the **Spirit**, unto obedience and sprinkling of the blood of **Jesus Christ**: Grace unto you, and peace, be multiplied." 1 Peter 1:2 [lps].

"Peter encouraged his readers by his strong declaration that they were chosen ("elect") by God the Father. At one time, only the nation of Israel could claim to be God's chosen people; but through Christ, all believers – Jews, former Jews, and Gentiles – belong to God. Our salvation and security rest in the free and merciful choice of the almighty God, no trials or persecutions can rob us of the eternal life he gives to those who believe in him." – *Life Application Bible,* p. 2195.

We Are Complete In His Workmanship

"Saving is all His idea, and all His work. All we do is trust Him enough to let Him do it. It's God's Gift from start to finish! We don't play the major role. If we did, we'd probably go around bragging that we'd done the whole thing! No, we neither make nor save ourselves. God does both the making and saving. He creates each of us by Christ Jesus to join Him in the work He does, the good work He has gotten ready for us to do...." Ephesians 2:8-10 (THE MESSAGE).

The Supernatural Omnipresence Of God

WIND and air are invisible, but we believe they exist by what we can see. The effects of wind are both beneficial and destructive!

Controlled by a windmill, it is used to make electricity. But it also has tremendous force within storms to move great objects and do much damage! Jesus used the wind as an illustration to explain God's Super-natural power to *transform a person's spirit and soul from one's natural human birth to being Born Anew into His Spiritual Kingdom*. Jesus explained this Spiritual Birth to Nicodemius:

"A person's body is born from his human parents. But a person's spiritual life is born from the Spirit. Don't be surprised when I tell you, 'You must all be born again.' The wind blows where it wants to go. *You hear the wind blow. But you don't know where the wind comes from or where it is going. It is the same with every person who is born from the Spirit.*" John 3:6-8 (EB) [lps].

"Jesus explained that we cannot control the work of the Holy Spirit. He works in ways we cannot predict or understand. Just as you did not control your physical birth, so you cannot control your spiritual birth. It is a gift from God through the Holy Spirit." – *Life Application Bible,* p. 1802.

The Apostle Paul explains The Holy Spirit in this way to the First Century Believers. "The Spirit knows all things, even *the deep secrets of God*. It is like this: No one knows the thoughts that another person has. Only a person's spirit that lives in him knows his thoughts. It is the same with God. No one knows the thoughts of God. Only the Spirit of God knows God's thoughts. We did not receive the spirit of the world, but we received the Spirit that is from God. We received this Spirit so that we can know all that God has given us." 1 Corinthians 2:10b - 12 (EB) [lps].

The "deep things [*secrets mentioned above*] of God*" are Jesus' resurrection and God's plan of salvation, revealed only to those who believe that what God says is true*. Those who believe in the resurrection and put their faith in Christ will know all they need to know to be saved. The knowledge, however, can't be grasped by even the wisest people unless they accept God's message. All who reject God's message are foolish, no matter how wise the world thinks they are." – *Life Application Bible,* p. 1999 [lps].

"The spiritual man tries all things [he examines investigates, inquires into, questions, and discerns all things], yet is himself to be put on trial and judged by no one [he can read the meaning of everything,

> Even though invisible, like the wind and the air we breathe, we can believe God's Holy Spirit is everywhere all the time, and is accessible to us if we are willing to receive Him and His Counselings!

but no one can properly discern or appraise or get an insight into him]. For who has known or understood the mind (the counsels and purposes) of the Lord so as to guide and instruct Him and give Him knowledge? But *we have the mind of Christ (the Messiah) and do hold the thoughts (feelings and purposes) of His heart*." 1 Corinthians 2:15-16 (Amp.) [lps].

When Examining Spiritual Truth

▸ Challenge what you know!
▸ Challenge what you think you know!
▸ Challenge what others say they know!
▸ Challenge what you have studied and the differences you have found through individual study!
▸ Timing is best suited when configuring that Truth comes slow, then firm, then sound, then fine, then sure, and finally refined to be incomparably realized!
▸ Acquiring valuable information makes profound changes to having excellence within and throughout one's lifespan!

God's Supernatural Transforming Power

 A LL nature reproduces after its kind, but it seems that God made the butterfly different to help us realize that it is possible to have a complete change of appearance as we realize that the butterfly didn't always have beautiful wings enabling it to fly!

Instead it came into this world as a caterpillar worm; spun a cocoon on a twig; and in God's Supernatural timing bursted forth as a butterfly!

God performs this same miraculous transformation upon every child, man and woman *who allows Him to transform their natural-born sinful nature into a Born-Anew Spiritual Son and Daughter* to His Praise, Honor and Glory.

The Apostle Paul wrote to the Believers in Corinth: "Therefore if any person is [ingrafted] in Christ (the Messiah) *he is a new creation* (a new creature altogether); the old [previous moral and spiritual condition] has passed away. Behold, the fresh and new has come!" 2 Corinthians 5:17 (Amp.) [lps].

"Christians are brand new people on the inside. The Holy Spirit gives them new life, and they are not the same anymore. We are not reformed, rehabilitated, or reeducated – we are new creations, living in vital union with Christ (Colossians 2:6, 7). We are not merely turning over a new leaf, we are *beginning a new life under a new Master*" – *Life Application Bible,* p. 2036 [lps].

"As you received Christ Jesus the Lord, so continue to live in him. *Keep your roots deep in him and have your lives built on him*. Be strong in the faith, just as you were taught. And always be thankful. *Be sure that no one leads you away with false ideas and words that mean nothing*. Those ideas come from men. They are the worthless ideas of this world. They are not from Christ. All of God lives in Christ fully [even when Christ was on earth]. And in him you have a full and true life. He is ruler over all rulers and powers." Colossians 2:6-10 (EB) [lps].

"Accepting Christ as Lord of your life is the beginning of life with Christ. But you must continue to follow his leadership by being rooted, built up, and established in the faith. Every day he desires to guide you and help you with your daily problems. You can live for Christ by (1) committing your life and submitting your will to him (Romans 12:1, 2); (2) seeking to learn from him his life, and his teachings (3:16); and (3) recognizing the Holy Spirit's power in you (Acts 1:8, Galatians 5:22). Paul used the illustration of our *being rooted in or connected to Christ. As plants draw nourishment from the soil through their roots, so we draw our life-giving strength from Christ*. The more we draw our life from him, the less we will be fooled by those who falsely claim to have life's answers (2;8)." – *Life Application Bible,* p. 2100 [lps].

Thought To Ponder
▸ Some church denominations attest to "do your best" because [they] will not accept anything besides or less to meet [their] so-called standards. However, it is far better to check out God's never changing and never ending Truth and Individual Plan for your own life as His Workmanship within you; thus allowing His Excellencies to transform you according to His Higher Standard as complete in your Relationship of the More Excellent Way, Truth and Life with His Graceful Divine Majestic encountering your whole lifetime through and through by redeeming your soul which is worth more than fine gold!

God's Powerful Protection And Care

A bird watcher recalls observing a threatening snake climbing a tree towards a bird's nest in the hope of getting a good meal. But each time he did so, a little mother bird attacked him at each eye with her beak and forced the snake to the ground! After putting the snake outstretched on  its way, the little mother bird resisted the snake not to return by picking its skin time after time, making the snake afraid to return because by this time it was bleeding all over!

In relating the incident to a friend, the bird watcher mentioned how much it reminded him of God's powerful, protecting care – of those who put their trust in Him – when Satan attempts to discourage or hurt one of His Children. And so for the Christian, we each are reminded to: "*Resist the devil* [stand firm against him], and he will flee from you." James 4:7 (Amp.) [lps].

Jesus also reminded His Followers: "Don't worry about the food you need to live. And don't worry about the clothes you need for your body. Life is more important than food. And the body is more important than clothes. *Look at the birds in the air*. They don't plant or harvest or store food in barns. But *your heavenly Father feeds the birds*. And *you know that you are worth*  *much more than the birds*. You cannot add any time to your life by worrying about it.... The thing you should *want most is God's kingdom and doing what God wants*. Then all these other things you need will be given to you. So don't worry about tomorrow. Each day has enough trouble of its own. Tomorrow will have its own worries." Matthew 6:25-27; 33-34 (EB) [lps].

Jesus went on to say in this same sermon: "And why do you worry about clothes? *Look at the flowers in the field. See how they grow. They don't work or make clothes for themselves*. But I tell you that even Solomon with his riches was not dressed as beautifully as one of these flowers. God clothes the grass in the field like that. The grass is living today, but tomorrow it is thrown into the fire to be burned. So *you can be even more sure that God will clothe you....*" Matthew 6:28-30 (EB) [lps].

"Because of the ill effects of worry, Jesus tells us to 'take no thought' about those needs that God promises to supply. Worry may (1) damage your health, (2) cause the object of your worry to consume your thoughts, (3) disrupt your productivity, (4) negatively affect the way you treat others, and (5) reduce your ability to trust in God. How many ill effects of worry are you experiencing? *Here is the difference between worry and genuine concern* – worry immobilizes, but concern moves you to action. *To seek 'first the kingdom of God, and his righteousness'* means to *turn to him first for help*, to fill your thoughts with his desire, to take his character for your pattern, and to serve and obey him in everything. What is really important to you? People, objects, goals, and other desires all compete for priority. Any of these can quickly bump God out of first place if you don't actively choose to give him first place in every area of your life. Planning for tomorrow is time well spent; worrying about tomorrow is time wasted. Sometimes it's difficult to tell the difference. Careful planning is thinking ahead about goals, steps, and schedules, and trusting in God's guidance. *When done well, planning can help alleviate worry*. The worrier, by contrast, is consumed by fear and finds it difficult to trust God. The worrier lets his plans interfere with his relationship with God." – *Life Application Bible,* pp. 1568-1569 [lps].

Thought To Ponder

▸ Be assured, God intends for us to use physical means of strength that He has empowered us with to bring about the necessities of food, clothing and shelter! See Galatians 6:5; 1 Thessalonians 4:11; 1 Timothy 5:8.

Jesus Illustrated Spiritual Truths Through Nature

TO help His Followers understand the Spirit-Filled life in Him, Jesus compared it with a grapevine. He said: *"I am the true vine, and my Father is the farmer.* Every branch in me that doesn't bear fruit, he takes away. Every branch that bears fruit, he prunes, that it may bear more fruit. You are already pruned clean because of the word which I have spoken to you. *Remain in me, and I in you. As the branch can't bear fruit by itself, unless it remains in the vine, so neither can you, unless you remain in me.* I am the vine. You are the branches. He who remains in me, and I in him, the same bears much fruit, for apart from me you can do nothing. If a man doesn't remain in me, he is thrown out as a branch, and is withered; and they gather them, throw them into the fire, and they are burned. *If you remain in me, and my words remain in you, you will ask whatever you desire, and it will be done for you. In this is my Father glorified, that you bear much fruit;* and so you will be my disciples. Even as the Father has loved me, I also have loved you. Remain in my love. If you keep my commandments, you will remain in my love; even as I have kept my Father's commandments, and remain in his love. I have spoken these things to you, that my joy may remain in you, and that your joy may be made full. *This is my commandment, that you love one another,* even as I have loved you. Greater love has no one than this, that someone lay down his life for his friends. You are my friends, if you do whatever I command you. No longer do I call you servants, for the servant doesn't know what his lord does. But I have called you friends, for everything that I heard from my Father, I have made known to you. *You didn't choose me, but I chose you, and appointed you, that you should go and bear fruit, and that your fruit should remain;* that whatever you will ask of the

Father in my name, he may give it to you. I command these things to you, that you may love one another. If the world hates you, you know that it has hated me before it hated you. If you were of the world, the world would love its own. But because you are not of the world, since I chose you out of the world, therefore the world hates you. Remember the word that I said to you: 'A servant is not greater than his lord.' If they persecuted me, they will also persecute you. If they kept my word, they will keep yours also. But all these things will they do to you for my name's sake, because they don't know him who sent me. If I had not come and spoken to them, they would not have had sin; but now they have no excuse for their sin. He who hates me, hates my Father also. If I hadn't done among them the works which no one else did, they wouldn't have had sin. But now have they seen and also hated both me and my Father. But this happened so that the word may be fulfilled which was written in their law, 'They hated me without a cause.' When the Counselor has come, whom I will send to you from the Father, the Spirit of truth, who proceeds from the Father, he will testify about me. You will also testify, because you have been with me from the beginning." John 15:1-17 (WEB).

"Many people try to do good, be honest, and do what is right. But *Jesus says the only way to live a truly good life is to stay close to him*, like a branch attached to the vine. Apart from him our efforts are unfruitful. Are you receiving the nourishment and life offered by Christ, the vine? If not, you are missing a special gift he has for you." – *Life Application Bible*, p. 1840 [lps].

"Fruit" does not necessarily mean soul-winning and other phases of ministry. The Apostle Peter describes Spiritual Growth in this manner.

"Jesus has the power of God. *His power has given us everything we need to live and to serve God*. We have these things because we know him. Jesus called us by his glory and goodness. *Through his glory and goodness, he gave us the very great and rich gifts he promised us.* With those gifts you can share in being like God. And so the world will not ruin you with its evil desires. Because you have these blessings, you should try as much as you can to add these things to your lives: to your *faith*, add *goodness*; and to your goodness, add *knowledge*; and to your knowledge, add *self-control*; and to your self-control, add the *ability to hold on*; and to your ability to hold on, add *service for God*; and to your service for God, add *kindness* for your brothers and sisters in Christ; and to this kindness, add *love*. If *all these things are in you and are growing*, they will help you never to be useless. They will help your knowledge of our Lord Jesus Christ make your lives better." 2 Peter 1:3-8 (EB) [lps].

The three essential elements needed for vegetational growth is the proper amount of pH in the soil, sunlight, and water for each species – which can be likened to the Trinity Who gives Vibrant Life and continual Spiritual Growth to every Born-Anew Believer in Christ!

The Fruit Of The Spirit

"The fruit of the [Holy] Spirit [the work which His presence within accomplishes] is *love, joy* (gladness), *peace, patience* (an even temper, forbearance), *kindness, goodness* (benevolence), *faithfulness, gentleness* (meekness, humility), *self-control* (self-restraint, continence). Against such things there is no law [that can bring a charge]." Galatians 5:22-23 (Amp.) [lps].

JESUS *used stories to teach them* [His Followers] many things. He said: 'A farmer went out to plant his seed. While he was planting, some *seed fell by the road*. The birds came and ate all that seed. Some seed *fell on rocky ground*, where there wasn't enough dirt. That seed grew very fast, because the ground was not deep. But when the sun rose, the plants dried up because they did not have deep roots. Some other seed *fell among thorny weeds*. The weeds grew and choked the good plants. Some other seed *fell on good ground where it grew and became grain*. Some plants made 100 times more grain. Other plants made 60 times more grain, and some made 30 times more grain. ... So listen to the *meaning of that story* about the farmer. What is the seed that fell by the *road*? That seed is like the person who hears the teaching about the kingdom but *does not understand it.* The Evil One comes and takes away the things that were planted in that person's heart. And what is the seed that fell on *rocky ground*? That seed is like the person who hears the teaching and quickly accepts it with joy. But he does not let the teaching go deep into his life. He keeps it only a short time. When *trouble or persecution comes because of the teaching he accepted, then he quickly gives up.* And what is the seed like that fell among the *thorny weeds*? That seed is like the person who hears the teaching but lets worries about this life and love of money stop that teaching from growing. So the teaching does not produce fruit in that person's life. But what is the seed that fell on the *good ground*. That seed is like the person who *hears the teaching and understands it. That person grows and produces fruit*, sometimes 100 times more, sometimes 60 times more, and sometimes 30 times more.'" Matthew 16:1-9, 18-23 (EB) [lps]. "The *four types of soil represent different responses to God's message*. People respond differently because they are in different states of readiness. Some are hardened, others are shallow, others are contaminated by distracting cares, and some are receptive. *How has God's Word taken root in your life? What kind of soil are you?*" – *Life Application Bible,* p. 1588 [lps].

THEN Jesus told another story: 'The *kingdom of heaven* is like a mustard *seed*. A man plants the seed in his field. That seed is the smallest of all seeds. But when it *grows*, it is one of the largest garden plants. It becomes a tree, big enough for the wild birds to come and make nests in its branches.'" Matthew 13:31-32 (EB) [lps].

"The mustard seed was the smallest seed a farmer used. Jesus used this parable to show that the Kingdom has small beginnings but will grow and produce great results." – *Life Application Bible,* p. 1589.

AT another time Jesus again talked about a mustard seed when His Disciples ask Him to increase their faith. He answered: "If you had faith (trust and confidence in God) even [so small] like a grain of mustard seed, you could say to this mulberry tree, Be pulled up by the roots, and be planted in the sea, and it would obey you." Luke 18:6 (Amp.) By this answer, Jesus was assuring the Disciples that it isn't the amount of faith, but the *right kind of faith that counts with God*.

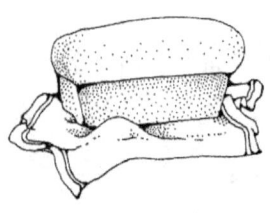

THEN Jesus told another story: 'The *kingdom of heaven is like yeast* that a woman mixes into a big bowl of flour. The yeast makes all the dough rise.' Jesus used stories to tell all these things to the people. He always used stories to teach people This is as the prophet said: 'I will speak using stories; I will tell things that have been secret since the world was made.'" Matthew 13:33-35 (EB) [lps].

"In other Bible passages, leaven (yeast) is used as a symbol of evil or uncleanness. Here it is a *positive symbol of growth*. Although yeast looks like a minor ingredient, it permeates the whole loaf. *Although the Kingdom began small and was nearly invisible, it would soon grow and have a great impact on the world*." – *Life Application Bible,* p. 1589 [lps].

THEN Jesus told them this story: 'Suppose one of you has 100 sheep, but he loses 1 of them. Then he will leave the other 99 sheep alone and go out and *look for the lost sheep*. The man will keep on searching for the lost sheep until he finds it. And when he finds it, the man is very happy. He puts it on his shoulders and goes home. He calls to his friends and neighbors and says, "Be happy with me because *I found my lost sheep!*" In the same way, I tell you there is *much joy in heaven when 1 sinner changes his heart*. There is more joy for that 1 sinner than there is for 99 good people who don't need to change."' Luke 15:3-7 (EB) [lps].

"Because each sheep was of high value, the shepherd knew it was worthwhile to search diligently for the lost one. *God's love for each individual is so great that he seeks each one out and rejoices when he or she is 'found.'* Jesus associated with sinners because he wanted to bring the lost sheep – people considered beyond hope – the Gospel of God's Kingdom. *Before you were a believer he sought you, and his love is still seeking those who are yet lost*. We can perhaps understand a God who would forgive sinners who come to him for mercy, but a *God who tenderly searches for sinners and then joyfully forgives them must have extraordinary love!* This is the kind of love that prompted Jesus to come to earth to search for lost people and save them. This is the kind of extraordinary love God has for you. If you feel far from God, don't despair. He is searching for you." – *Life Application Bible, p.* 1759 [lps].

Thoughts To Ponder
- "Yes, *I have loved you with an everlasting love*; therefore with loving-kindness have I drawn you and continued My faithfulness to you." Jeremiah 31:3 (Amp.) [lps].
- "See what [an incredible] *quality of love the Father has given* (shown, bestowed on) *us*, that we should [be permitted to] be named and called and counted the children of God! And so we are...!" 1 John 3:1 (Amp.) [lps].

God's Supernatural Surpasses The Natural

IN this chapter we will consider a few instances recorded in the Old Testament Scriptures where God manifested His Supernatural Power over and beyond nature in behalf of humankind.

God had directed *Moses* to deliver the people of Israel from Egyptian bondage and move them to another place. The Pharaoh (King) of Egypt didn't want to release the Israelites at first, but then said they could go. When the Israelites were all out in the desert with mountains on each side and the Red Sea in front of them, they saw that the Egyptian Army was approaching – and they were very frightened! But Moses said to them: "'*Don't be afraid! Stand still and see the Lord save you today*. You will never see these Egyptians again after today. You will only need to remain calm. The Lord will fight for you.' Then the Lord said to Moses, 'Why are you crying out to me? Command the people of Israel to start moving. *Raise your walking stick and hold it over the sea. The sea will split*. Then the people can cross the sea on dry land. I have made the Egyptians stubborn so they will chase the Israelites. But I will be honored when I defeat the king and all of his chariot drivers and chariots.... Then Egypt will know that I am the Lord.' The angel of God usually traveled in front of Israel's army. Now the angel of God moved behind them. Also, the pillar of cloud moved from in front of the people and stood behind them. So the cloud came between the Egyptians and the people of Israel. The cloud made it dark for the Egyptians. But it gave light to the Israelites. So the cloud kept the two armies apart all night. *Moses held his hand over the sea. All that night the Lord drove back the sea with a strong east wind*. And so he made the *sea become dry ground*. The *water was split*. And *the Israelites went through the sea on dry land*. A wall of water was on both sides. Then all the king's horses, chariots and chariot drivers followed them into the sea. Between two and six o'clock in the morning, the Lord looked down from the pillar of cloud and fire at the Egyptian army. He made them panic. He kept the wheels of the chariots from turning. This made it hard to drive the chariots. The Egyptians shouted, 'Let's get away from the Israelites! The Lord is fighting for them and against us Egyptians.' Then the Lord told Moses, '*Hold your hand over the sea. Then the water will come back over the Egyptians*, their chariots and chariot drivers.' So *Moses raised his hand over the sea. And at dawn the water became deep again. The Egyptians were trying to run from it. But the Lord swept them away into the sea*. The water became deep again. It covered the chariots and chariot drivers. So all the king's army that had followed the Israelites into the sea was covered. Not one of them survived." Exodus 14:13-28 (EB) [lps].

What a story of God's intervention in behalf of His People! Believers living today can be sure God can and will still manifest His Supernatural Power in behalf of those who trust in Him!

Thoughts To Ponder

▸ Do you have attitudes, which may be called enemies, within your own spirit and soul today that threaten your peace: e.g., fear, anxiety, worry, anger, envy, doubt, hate, and/or others _____, _____ ? If so, follow God instructions to be *"still and see the Lord save [YOU] today;"* by allowing Him to destroy any and all of them in the *depths of YOUR sea of trouble* as He did with the Egyptian Army centuries ago, and others since then who realize their need of His Supernatural Power which far surpasses all nature and natural sin-born inclinations!

▸ "In [this] freedom Christ has made us free [and completely liberated us] stand fast then, and *do not be hampered and held ensnared and submit again to a yoke of slavery* [which you have once put off]." Galatians 5:1 (Amp.) [lps].

ANOTHER incident of God's Supernatural Power over nature is when the Prophet Daniel was thrown into the lions' den for praying to the True God of Heaven, but was kept safe from their hungry jaw! Israel  had been invaded by Nebuchadnezzar, King of Babylon, and took the most strong, healthy, and educated young men to his palace to be trained for three years in their language and royal leadership. At the end of three years, Daniel and three other Israelite young men excelled higher than any of the other young men who went through the same training, and Daniel was given a high position in the King's Palace. When Darius the Mede invaded the country and became the new King, he promoted Daniel to be one of three supervisors who were over 120 governors.

Jealousy burned in the hearts of some of Darius' administrators against Daniel and they persuaded the King to make a degree that no one was to pray to any god or man except to the King for 30 days; because they knew Daniel had a habit of praying to the God of Heaven three times a day in an open window facing Jerusalem. The punishment would be that the person who violated the law would be thrown into the lions' den which was kept for criminals. When the jealous men saw Daniel violating the King's law, they quickly reported him to Darius. Darius was saddened because he appreciated and respected Daniel. When he put Daniel in the lions' den, he said: "*May the God you serve all the time save you!*" Daniel 6:16 (EB) [lps].

The next morning King Darius rushed to the lions' den and called: "'*Daniel, servant of the living God! Has your God that you always worship been able to save you from the lions*?' Daniel answered, 'My king, live forever! *My God sent his angel to close the lions' mouths*. They have not hurt me because my God knows I am innocent. I never did anything wrong to you, my king.' King Darius was very happy. He told his servants to lift Daniel out of the lions' den. So they lifted him out and did not find any injury on him. This was because Daniel had trusted in his God. Then the *king gave a command The men who had accused Daniel were brought to the lions' den and thrown into it. Their wives and children were also thrown into it. The lions grabbed them before they hit the floor of the den. And the lions crushed their bones.* Then King Darius wrote a letter. It was to all people and all nations, to those who spoke every language in the world: 'I wish you great wealth. I am making a new law. This law is for people in every part of my kingdom. All of you must fear and respect the God of Daniel. Daniel's God is the living God. He lives forever. *His kingdom will never be destroyed. His rule will never end. God rescues and saves people. God does mighty miracles in heaven and on earth*. God saved Daniel from the power of the lions.' So Daniel was successful during the time that Darius was king. This was also the time that Cyrus the Persian was king." Daniel 6:19b - 28 (EB) [lps].

Thoughts To Ponder
▸ In addition to being a trustworthy administrator under four Kings in a foreign land, God graced Daniel in giving him Spiritual understanding in visions and dreams which spanned a time frame of almost 600 years ending in AD 70.
▸ His "book concludes with a series of visions which Daniel had during the reigns of Belshazzar (chapters 7, 8), Darius (chapter 9), and Cyrus (chapters 10-12).... They give a preview of God's redemption and have been called the key to all biblical prophecy. God is sovereign. He was in control in Babylon, and he has been moving in history, controlling the destinies of people ever since. And he is here now! *Despite news reports or personal stress, we can be confident that God is in control*. As you read Daniel, watch God work and *find your security in his sovereignty*." – *Life Application Bible,* p. 1407.
▸ These dreams dramatically outlined God's Plans *of the then of there,* beginning with Babylon and continuing to the end of the Jewish Age in AD 70.

DANIEL'S three friends who had also been captured by King Nebuchadnezzar and trained in his Royal Palace, eventually were promoted over the province of Babylon. Their names were Shadrach, Meshach, and Abednego.

The King had made a gold statue 90 feet tall and 9 feet wide. He gathered all his Government Officials to a great celebration. The announcer said, "When the music begins, everyone must bow and worship this gold statue." All bowed and worshiped the statue except Shadrach, Meshach, and Abednego! When the King heard that these three men didn't bow and worship the image he was furious! The King offered to play the music again and give the men another chance to bow and worship the image. He went on to say, "'If you do not worship it, you will be thrown quickly into the blazing  furnace. Then no god will be able to save you from my power.'" Daniel 3:15 (EB).

They replied, "You can throw us into the blazing furnace. The *God we serve is able to save us from the furnace* and your power. If he does this, it is good. *But even if God does not save us*, we want you, our king, to know this: *We will not serve your gods*. We will not worship the gold statue you have set up.'" Daniel 3:17-18 (EB) [lps].

The King ordered the furnace to be turned up seven times hotter. The soldiers left all the clothes on the three men, tied them with rope, and threw them into the blazing furnace! The fire was so hot it killed the soldiers who threw them in! Then the King was surprised, and jumped up! "'Didn't we tie up only three men? Didn't we throw them into the fire?' They answered, 'Yes, our king.' The king said, 'Look! I see four men. *They are walking around in the fire. They are not tied up, and they are not burned*. The fourth man looks like a son of the gods.'" Daniel 3:24-25 (EB) [lps]. Then the King called to the three men and told them to come out of the fire. All their clothes were still on them, and they didn't even smell like smoke! Gratefully the King said, "'Praise the God of Shadrach, Meshach and Abednego. *Their God has sent his angel and saved his servants from the fire*! These three men trusted their God. They refused to obey my command. And *they were willing to die rather than serve or worship any god other than their own*.'" Daniel 3:28 (EB) [lps].

Thoughts To Ponder
- "*Why didn't the men just bow to the image and tell God that they didn't mean it?* They had determined never to worship another god and they courageously took their stand. As a result, they were condemned and led away to be executed. They did not know whether they would be delivered from the fire, all they knew was that they would not bow to an idol. *Are you ready to take a stand for God no matter what?* When you stand for God, you will stand out. It may be painful, and it may not always have a happy ending. Be prepared to say, 'If he delivers me, *or* if he doesn't, I will serve only God.'" – *Life Application Bible,* p. 1415 [lps].
- "The three men had one more chance. Here are eight *excuses they could have used* to bow to the statue and save their lives: (1) We will bow down but not actually worship the idol. (2) We won't become idol worshipers, but will do this one time, then ask God for forgiveness. (3) The king has absolute power and we must obey him. God will understand. (4) The king appointed us – we owe this to him. (5) This is a foreign land so God will excuse us for following the customs of this land. (6) Our ancestors set up idols in God's Temple! This isn't half as bad! (7) We're not hurting anybody. (8) If we get ourselves killed and some heathens take our high positions, they won't help our people in exile!" – *Life Application Bible,* p. 1415 [lps].
- "*Although all these excuses sound sensible at first, they are dangerous*. To bow to the image would violate God's command." – *Life Application Bible,* p. 1415 [lps].

OUR last illustration in this chapter of how God's Supernatural surpasses the natural is a story of why *God spoke through a donkey* in a man's voice and language which is truly remarkable!

The people of Israel were on the borders of the Promised Land which they had been waiting to enter for 40 years! They were near the country of Moab, and King Balak was fearful of them. So he sent messengers to *Balaam who was a false prophet bribing him to come to a certain place to curse the people of Israel.* Even though Balaam was a false prophet, *he did have some knowledge of the True God of Heaven but was not totally committed to Him.* That night God spoke to Balaam saying he shouldn't go with them to curse the Israelites because HE had already blessed them! So the next morning Balaam said he couldn't go with them. Balak sent other messengers and the second time they came, *God said to Balaam, "Go. But only do what I tell you."*

"Balaam got up the next morning. He put a saddle on his donkey. Then he went with the Moabite leaders. But God became angry because Balaam went. Balaam was riding his donkey. And he had two servants with him. *The donkey saw the angel of the Lord standing in the road. The angel had a sword in his hand.* So the donkey left the road and went into the field. Balaam hit the donkey to force her back on the road. Later, the angel of the Lord stood on a narrow path between two vineyards. There were walls on both sides. Again the donkey saw the angel of the Lord. So the donkey walked close to one wall. This crushed Balaam's foot against the wall. So he hit her again. The angel of the Lord went ahead again. The angel stood at a narrow place. It was too narrow to turn left or right. The donkey saw the angel of the Lord. So she lay down under Balaam. Balaam was very angry and hit her with his stick. Then *the Lord made the donkey talk.* She said to Balaam,

'What have I done to make you hit me three times?' Balaam answered the donkey, 'You have made me look foolish! I wish I had a sword in my hand! I would kill you right now!' But the donkey said to Balaam. 'I am your very own donkey. You have ridden me for years. Have I ever done this to you before?' *Then the Lord let Balaam see the angel*. The angel of the Lord was *standing in the road with his sword drawn*. Then Balaam bowed facedown on the ground. The angel of the Lord asked Balaam, 'Why have you hit your donkey three times? I have stood here to stop you. What you are doing is wrong. The donkey saw me. She turned away from me three times. If she had not turned away, I would have killed you by now. But I would let her live.' Then Balaam said to the angel of the Lord, 'I have sinned. I did not know you were standing in the road to stop me. If I am wrong, I will go back.' The *angel of the Lord said to Balaam, 'Go with these men. But say only what I tell you*.' So Balaam went with Balak's leaders." Numbers 22:21-35 (EB) [lps].

Balak took Balaam to three different locations to view the Israelites camp and curse them; but *each time God caused Balaam to say blessings in behalf of the people of Israel instead of curses*! Balak was furious and said to Balaam, "'I called you here to curse my enemies. But you have blessed them three times. Now go home! I said I would pay you well. But the Lord has made you lose your reward.'" Numbers 24:10 (EB) [lps].

Thoughts To Ponder
- "Although Balak had hired Balaam to curse the Israelites, he got a blessing instead (Numbers 2:6, 12). *This demonstrates the hidden power of God in history. God's purposes are worked out even by people and nations who do not serve him*. Because we love and serve God, we can be confident that he will guide our paths. Let us keep our eyes open for his leading." – *Life Application Bible,* p. 277 [lps].
- Have you ever been offered money to do something you knew would not be to God's Praise, Honor and Glory?

Symbols Referring To Jesus The Christ

JESUS THE CHRIST is described through-out the Bible with almost 200 meaningful names, titles, offices, and symbols. God didn't hide His Signature from anything in nature, including humankind's intuitive acclivities, proclivities and declivities; so that people could be constantly reminded of His Unseen Presence, Love and Care through His Prevenient Grace!

Light Of Life

Jesus said, "I am the *light of the world*. The person who follows me will never live in darkness. He will have the *light that gives life*." John 8:12 (EB) [lps].

"Jesus was speaking in the part of the Temple known as the treasury (John 8:20), where *candles burned to symbolize the pillar of fire that led the people of Israel through the wilderness* (Exodus 13:21, 22)). In this context, Jesus called himself the *Light of the world.* The pillar of fire represented God's presence, protection, and guidance." – *Life Application Bible,* p. 1819.

All Born-Anew Believers are also the "*light of the world*" (Matthew 5:14); since the "Kingdom of God" dwells within them (Luke 17:21).

Living Water

When Jesus talked to a Samaritan woman at Jacob's Well, He said: "If you had only known and had recognized God's gift and Who this is that is saying to you, Give Me a drink, you would have asked Him [instead] and He would have given you

living water.... All who drink of this water will be thirsty again. But whoever takes a drink of the water that I will give him shall never, no never, be thirsty any more. But the *water that I will give him shall become a spring of water welling up (flowing, bubbling) [continually] within him unto (into, for) eternal life.*" John 4:10, 13-14) (Amp.) [lps].

"What did Jesus mean by 'living water?' In the Old Testament, many verses speak of thirsting after God as one thirsts for water (Psalm 42:1, Isaiah 55:1; Jeremiah 2:13; Zechariah 13:1). God is called *the fountain of life* (Psalm 36:9) and the *fountain of living waters* (Jeremiah 17:13). In saying he would bring living water that could forever quench one's thirst for God, Jesus was claiming to be the Messiah. *Only the Messiah could give this gift that satisfies the soul's desire.*" – *Life Application Bible,* p. 1805 [lps].

Bread
Jesus also likened Himself to bread.

"After these things, Jesus went away to the other side of the sea of Galilee, which is also called the Sea of Tiberias. A great multitude followed him, because they saw his signs which he did on those who were sick. Jesus went up into the mountain, and he sat there with his disciples. Now the Passover, the feast of the Jews, was at hand. Jesus therefore lifting up his eyes, and seeing that a great multitude was coming to him, said to Philip, "Where are we to buy bread, that these may eat?" This he said to test him, for he himself knew what he would do. Philip answered him, "Two hundred denarii worth of bread is not sufficient for them, that everyone of them may receive a little." One of his disciples, Andrew, Simon Peter's brother, said to him, "There is a boy here who has five barley loaves and two fish, but what are these among so many?" Jesus said, "Have the people sit down." Now there was much grass in that place. So the *men sat down, in number about five thousand. Jesus took the loaves; and having given thanks, he distributed to the disciples, and the disciples to those who were sitting down; likewise also of the fish as much as they desired.* When they were filled,

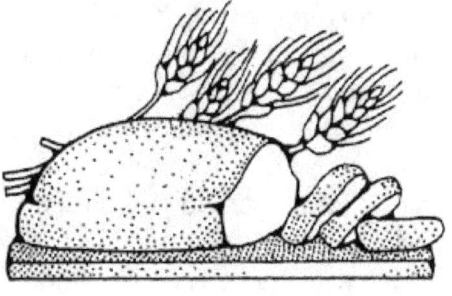

he said to his disciples, "Gather up the broken pieces which are left over, that nothing be lost." So they gathered them up, and filled twelve baskets with broken pieces from the five barley loaves, which were left over by those who had eaten. When therefore *the people saw the sign which Jesus did, they said, "This is truly the prophet who comes into the world."* Jesus therefore, perceiving that they were about to come and take him by force, to make him king, withdrew again to the mountain by himself. When evening came, his disciples went down to the sea, and they entered into the boat, and were going over the sea to Capernaum. It was now dark, and Jesus had not come to them. The sea was tossed by a great wind blowing. When therefore they had rowed about twenty-five or thirty stadia, they saw Jesus walking on the sea, and drawing near to the boat; and they were afraid. But he said to them, "It is I. Don't be afraid." They were willing therefore to receive him into the boat. Immediately the boat was at the land where they were going. On the next day, the multitude that stood on the other side of the sea saw that there was no other boat there, except the one in which his disciples had embarked, and that Jesus hadn't entered with his disciples into the boat, but his disciples had gone away alone. However boats from Tiberias came near to the place where they ate the bread after the Lord had given thanks. When the multitude therefore saw that Jesus wasn't there, nor his disciples, they themselves got into the boats, and came to Capernaum, seeking Jesus. When they found him on the other side of the sea, they asked him, "Rabbi, when did you come here?" Jesus answered them, "Most certainly I tell you, *you seek me, not because you saw signs, but because you ate of the loaves, and were filled. Don't work for the food which perishes, but for the food which remains to eternal life, which the Son of Man will give to you*. For God the Father has sealed him." They said therefore to him, "What must we do, that we may work the works of God?" Jesus answered them, "This is the work of God, that you believe in him whom he has sent." They said therefore to him, "What then do you do for a sign, that we may see, and believe you? What work do you do? Our fathers ate the manna in the wilderness. As it is written, 'He gave them bread out of heaven to eat.'" Jesus therefore said to them, "Most certainly, I tell you, it wasn't Moses who gave you the bread out of heaven, but *my Father gives you the true bread out of heaven*. For the *bread of God is that which comes down out of heaven, and gives life to the world.*" They said therefore to him, "Lord, always give us this bread." *Jesus said to them, "I am the bread of life. He who comes to me will not be hungry, and he who believes in me will never be thirsty*. But I told you that you have seen me, and yet you don't believe. All those whom the Father gives me will come to me. *He who comes to me I will in no way throw out.* For I have come down from heaven, not to do my own will, but the will of him who sent me. This is the will of my Father who sent me, that of all he has given to me I should lose nothing, but should raise him up at the last day. This is the will of the one who sent me, that everyone who sees the Son, and believes in him, should have eternal life; and I will raise him up at the last day." John 6:1-40 (WE B).

"People eat bread to satisfy physical hunger and to sustain physical life. We can satisfy spiritual hunger and sustain spiritual life only by a right relationship with Jesus Christ. No wonder he called himself the Bread of life. But *bread must be eaten* to give life and *Christ must be invited into our daily walk to give spiritual life*." – *Life Application Bible,* p. 1813 [lps].

Resurrection Plant

This plant is a name for several different kinds depending upon the arid region of where they grow. They have hygroscopic qualities causing them to curl up when dry and to unfold when moist. In the *dry stage, one would think the plant was dead*; but given water, it revives very rapidly into a live plant! Just so – spiritually speaking – *we may experience areas in our lives which seem dry as a desert; but at those times we are to be still and know that God is at work for the proper timings, so that He can renew us for our next season*!

Bright Morning Star

"I Jesus, have sent my angel to testify these things to you for the assemblies. I am the root and the offspring of David; the **Bright and Morning Star**." Revelation 22:16 (WEB).

Morning Dew

"I will be like the **dew to Israel**. He will blossom like the lily, and send down his roots like Lebanon." Hosea 14:5 (WEB)

Sun of Righteousness

"But to you who fear my name shall the **sun of righteousness** arise with healing in its wings. You will go out, and leap like calves of the stall." Malachi 4:2 (WEB)

Lamb Of God

"The next day, he saw Jesus coming to him, and said, "Behold, the **Lamb of God**, who takes away the sin of the world!" John 1:29 (WEB)

Arm Of The Lord

"Who hath believed our report? and to whom is **the arm of the Lord** revealed?" Isaiah 53:1.

Spiritual Meat /Spiritual Rock

"Moreover, brethren, I would not that ye should be ignorant, how that all our fathers were under the cloud, and all passed through the sea; and were all baptized unto Moses in the cloud and in the sea; and did all **eat the same spiritual meat; and did all drink the same spiritual drink:** for they drank of that spiritual Rock that followed them: and that **Rock was Christ**.' 1 Corinthians 10:1-4

Chief Corner Stone

"So then you are no longer strangers and foreigners, but you are fellow citizens with the saints, and of the household of God, being built on the foundation of the apostles and prophets, **Christ Jesus himself being the chief cornerstone;** in whom the whole building, **fitted together, grows into a holy** *temple in the Lord;* in whom you also are *built together for a habitation of God in the Spirit.*" Ephesians 2:19-22 (WEB)

Lion of the Tribe of Judah

"One of the elders said to me, "Don't weep. Behold, the *Lion who is of the tribe of Judah, the Root of David,* has overcome; he who opens the book and its seven seals." Revelation 5:5 (WEB)

Great Shepherd Of The Sheep

"Now may the God of peace, who brought again from the dead the *great shepherd of the sheep with the blood of an eternal covenant*, our Lord Jesus, make you complete in every good work to do his will, working in you that which is well pleasing in his sight, through Jesus Christ, to whom be the glory forever and ever. Amen." Hebrews 13:20-21 (WEB).

" The *Lord is my shepherd;* I shall not want. He maketh me to lie down in green pastures: he leadeth me beside the still waters. He restoreth my soul: he leadeth me in the paths of righteousness for his name's sake. Yea, though I walk through the valley of the shadow of death, I will fear no evil: for thou art with me; thy rod and thy staff they comfort me. Thou preparest a table before me in the presence of mine enemies: thou anointest my head with oil; my cup runneth over. Surely goodness and mercy shall follow me all the days of my life: and I will dwell in the house of the Lord for ever." Psalm 23'

"What do you think? If a man has *one hundred sheep, and one of them goes astray, doesn't he leave the ninety-nine, go to the mountains, and seek that which has gone astray?* If he finds it, most certainly I tell you, he rejoices over it more than over the ninety-nine which have not gone astray." Matthew 18:12-13 (WEB.

"Beware of false prophets, who come to you in sheep's clothing, but inwardly are ravening wolves." Matthew 7:15 (WEB).

"But when he saw the multitudes, he was moved with compassion for them, because they were harassed and scattered, like *sheep without a shepherd."* Matthew 9:36 (WEB).

"Behold, *I send you out as sheep among wolves.* Therefore be wise as serpents, and harmless as doves." Matthew 10:16 (WEB).

Both Shepherd And Door Of The Sheep Fold

"Most certainly, I tell you, one who doesn't enter by the *door into the sheep fold,* but climbs up some other way, the same is a thief and a robber. But one who *enters in by the door is the shepherd of the sheep.* The gatekeeper opens the gate for him, and the sheep listen to his voice. He *calls his own sheep by name, and leads them out.* Whenever he brings out his own sheep, he goes before them, and the sheep follow him, for they know his voice. They will by no means follow a stranger, but will flee from him; for they don't know the voice of strangers." Jesus spoke this parable to them, but they didn't understand what he was telling them. Jesus therefore said to them again, "Most certainly, I tell you, *I am the sheep's door.* All who came before me are thieves and robbers, but the sheep didn't listen to them. *I am the door. If anyone enters in by me, he will be saved, and will go in and go out, and will find pasture.* The thief only comes to steal, kill, and destroy. *I came that they may have life, and may have it abundantly.* I am the good shepherd. The *good shepherd lays down his life for the sheep.* He who is a hired hand, and not a shepherd, who doesn't own the sheep, *sees the wolf coming, leaves the sheep, and flees. The wolf snatches the sheep, and scatters them.* The hired hand flees because he is a hired hand, and doesn't care for the sheep. *I am the good*

shepherd. I know my own, and I'm known by my own; even as the Father knows me, and I know the Father. I lay down my life for the sheep. *I have other sheep,* which are not of this fold. I must bring them also, and they will hear my voice. They will become one flock with one shepherd. Therefore the Father loves me, because *I lay down my life, that I may take it again.* No one takes it away from me, but I lay it down by myself. I have power to lay it down, and I have power to take it again. I received this commandment from my Father." John 10:1-18 (WEB).

Radiance Of His Gory

"His Son is the *radiance of his glory,* the very image of his substance, and upholding all things by the word of his power, when he had by himself purified us of our sins, sat down on the right hand of the Majesty on high; having become so much better than the angels, as he has inherited a more excellent name than they have." Hebrews 1:3-4 (WEB).

Grace Taught My Heart To Believe - Romans 2:4
And Grace Shall Lead Me Home - Colossians 4:12
In, With, For, Through, Of, From and To The . . .

PLEASINGS TO ENJOINMENTS

Spirit of the Lord (Owner)

Spirit of Wisdom

Spirit of Understanding

Spirit of Counsel

Spirit of Might

Spirit of Knowledge

Spirit of the Fear of the Lord
(Godly Fear As Reverential Love)

FULFILLMENTINGS OF CHARACTERISTICS

Reminders Of Salvation Seen In Nature

THE Lord says, 'Come, we will talk these things over. Your *sins are red like deep red cloth*. But they can be as *white as snow*.'" Isaiah 1:18 (EB) [lps].

"A deep stain is virtually impossible to remove from clothing, and the stain of sin seems equally permanent. But *God can remove the stain of sin from our lives* as he promised to do for the Israelites. We don't have to go through life permanently soiled. If we are willing and obedient, God's Word assures us that Christ has forgiven and removed our most indelible stains." –

Life Application Bible, p. 1154 [lps].

"If we confess our sins, he is faithful and just to forgive our sins, and to *cleanse us from all unrighteousness*." 1 John 1:9 [lps].

"Confession is supposed to free us to enjoy fellowship with Christ. It should ease our consciences and lighten our cares. But some Christians do not understand how it works. They feel so guilty that they confess the same sins over and over, and then wonder if they might have forgotten something. Other Christians believe God forgives them when they confess, but if they died with unconfessed sins, they would be forever lost. These Christians do not understand that God wants to forgive us. He allowed his beloved Son to die just so he could pardon us. *When we come to Christ, he forgives all the sins we have committed or will ever commit*. We don't need to confess the sins of the past all over again, and we don't need to fear that he will cast us out if we don't keep our slate perfectly clear. Of course we want to continue to confess our sins, but not because we think failure to do so will make us lose our salvation. Our *hope in Christ is secure*. Instead, we confess so we can enjoy maximum fellowship and joy with him. *True confession also involved a commitment not to continue in sin*. We are not genuinely confessing our sins before God if we plan to commit the sin again and just want temporary forgiveness. We must pray for strength to defeat the temptation the next time it appears." – *Life Application Bible,* p. 2216 [lps].

GOD used a unique illustration to help people realize that they *cannot free themselves from yielding to temptation*. He said, "Can the Ethiopian change his skin or the *leopard his spots*? Then also can you do good who are accustomed and taught, even trained, to do evil." Jeremiah 13:23 (Amp) [lps].

When the Holy Spirit convicted King David of his sin, he prayed: "God, be merciful to me because you are loving. Because you are always ready to be merciful, wipe out all my wrongs. *Wash away all my guilt and make me clean again*. I know about my wrongs. I can't forget my sin. You are the one I have sinned against. I have done what you say is wrong. So you are right when you speak. You are fair when you judge me.... *Create in me a pure heart*, God. *Make my spirit right again*. Do not send me away from you. Do not take your Holy Spirit away from me. *Give me back the joy* that comes when you save me. *Keep me strong by giving me a willing spirit*. Then I will teach your ways to those who do wrong. And sinners will turn back to you." Psalm 51:1-4; 10-13 (EB) [lps].

I will greatly *rejoice in the Lord*, my soul will exult in my God; for He has clothed me with the garments of salvation. He has covered me with the robe of righteousness, as a bridegroom decks himself with a garland, and *as a bride adorns herself with her jewels*. For as [surely as] the *earth*

brings forth its shoots, and as a garden causes what is sown in it to spring forth, so [surely] the **Lord God will cause righteousness and justice and praise to spring forth** before all the nations [through the self-fulfilling power of His word]. Isaiah 61:10-11 (Amp.) [lps].

"The imagery of the **bridegroom** is often used in Scripture to depict the <u>Messiah</u> (see Matthew 9:15), while the imagery of the *bride* is used to depict <u>God's People</u> (see Revelation 19:6-8). **We too can be clothed with the righteousness of Christ when we believe in him** (2 Corinthians 5:21)." – *Life Application Bible,* p. 1227 [lps].

God's Righteousness Is Endued Within Every Believer

"For our sake He made Christ [virtually] to be sin Who knew no sin, so that in and through Him we might become [endued with, viewed as being in, and examples of] the righteousness of God [what we ought to be, approved and acceptable and in right relationship with Him, by His goodness]." 2 Corinthians 5:21 (Amp.) [lps].

"**When we trust in Christ, we make a trade – our sin for his goodness**. Our sin was poured into Christ at his crucifixion. His righteousness is poured into us at our conversion. This is what Christians mean by Christ's atonement for sin. In the world, bartering works only when two people exchange goods of relatively equal value. But ***God offers to trade his righteousness for our sin*** – something of immeasurable worth for something worthless. How grateful we should be for his goodness to us." – *Life Application Bible,* p. 2036 [lps].

Thought To Ponder
- ▸ "But of him are [you] in Christ Jesus, who of God is made unto us wisdom, and righteousness, and sanctification, and redemption." 1 Corinthians 1:30 [lps].

A cat lover tells the story of when God's Love was made more real to her as she watched a mother cat wrap her front arms (legs) around her young kittens and purr contentedly as she cuddled them close to herself. She went on to say, "Did you know the ***Bible says that God sings over us***?" Yes. That is what He does, dear reader. Notice these precious Words of Scripture: "The Lord your God is with you. The mighty One will save you. The Lord will be happy with you. You will rest in his love. ***He will sing and be joyful about you***." Zephaniah 3:17 (EB) [lps]. And here is more confirmation of God's Supernatural Love which far surpasses our comprehension. "Can a woman forget the baby she nurses? Can she feel no kindness for the child she gave birth to? Even if she could forget her children, ***I will not forget you***." Isaiah 49:15 (EB) [lps].

THE time was coming when Jesus' purpose on this earth was soon to close. As He looked upon His Beloved City of Jerusalem Jesus cried:

"Jerusalem, Jerusalem! You kill the prophets and kill with stones those men God sent to you. Many times I wanted to help your people! I wanted to gather them together ***as a hen gathers her chicks under her wings***. But you did not let me. Now your home will be left completely empty." Matthew 23:37 (EB) [lps].

"Jesus wanted to gather his people together as a hen protects her chicks under her wings, but they wouldn't let him. ***Jesus also wants to protect us if we will come to him***. Many times we hurt and don't know where to turn. We reject Christ's help because we don't think he can give us what we need. But who knows our needs better than our Creator? ***Those who turn to Jesus will find that he helps and comforts as no one else can***." – *Life Application Bible*, p. 1616 [lps].

Symbolic Language Used Throughout The Bible

AS we have discussed, our *Unseen*, Majestic, Supernatural God has revealed Himself to us through what *we see in nature*! But He is NOT nature, although He made all that is natural for humankind's benefit.

Parable – Luke 10:25-37
Fable – 2 Kings 14:8-10
Simile – Matthew 3:16
Metaphor – Matthew 26:26
Allegory – Ephesians 6:11-17
Riddle – Judges 14:14
Hyperbole – Psalm 22:6, 14
Irony – Matthew 27:29
Sarcasm – Mark 15:31-32
Interrogation – Hebrews 2:3
Metonymy – 1 Cor. 11:25-26
Personification – Psalm 114:3
Anthropomorphism – Ex. 33:22-23

But for the Deist, we Christians must direct everyone's attention further unto the *Unspeakable Gift* (2 Cor. 9:15); into the *Unspeakable Words* (2 Cor. 2:4); and onto the *Unspeakable Joy* (1 Peter 1:8). The above list of the various types of symbolic language found in God's Holy Word gives the reader spiritual insight as to Its True meaning. Therefore, *discernment is necessary to decipher what is literal and what is symbolic*; what is physical in one sense in the Old Covenant, and ends up in a spiritual sense in the New Covenant; and leaving the 'mixtures of the Two Covenants' by man-made divisives completely out!

Also, in studying the writings and prophecies of both the Old and New Covenants, it is important to ask yourself: WHO was speaking in this passage – and to WHOM?? under WHAT circumstances was it written – and WHERE?? WHY was the speaker/writer saying it or giving this prophecy – and WHEN?? The answer to these simple questions will help you understand the Bible more clearly and also help you realize that the prophecies given were for those Biblical times and not 2,000+ years in its future and to the intimidation of multitudes!

Peter describes the Old Covenant of rituals which came to an end at the destruction of Jerusalem by the Romans in AD

70: "But the day of the Lord will come as a thief in the night; in the which the heavens shall pass away with a great noise, and the *elements*[1] shall melt with fervent heat, the earth also and the works that are therein shall be burned up. Seeing then that all these things shall be dissolved, what manner of persons ought ye to be in all holy conversation and godliness. Looking for and hasting unto the coming of the day of God, wherein the heavens being on fire shall be dissolved, and the elements shall melt with fervent heat? Nevertheless *we,*[2] according to His promise, look for new heavens and a new earth, wherein dwelleth *righteousness.*[3] Wherefore, *beloved,*[4] seeing that ye look for such things, be diligent that ye may be found of Him in peace, without spot, and blameless." 2 Peter 3:10-14 [lps]. *The Day Of The Lord mentioned in the Old Testament meant the destruction of a nation by the power of God working through human armies*: "For the day of the Lord of hosts shall be upon every one that is proud and lofty, and upon every one that is lifted up; and he shall be brought low." Isaiah 2:12. The next chapter gives a comparison between the apocalyptic language used in the Old and New Testaments.

---

[1] Biblical meaning for elements is principles/rudiments/ordinances. See Gal. 4:1-5; 9-10; Col. 2:8, 20-22; Heb. 5:12-14. The "elements" are emblematic for the Old Covenant of works and rituals which were quickly coming to an end for the Jewish "world" of worship (AD 70 when Jerusalem was destroyed). This verse DOES NOT mean the end of this physical world (cosmos) which is being preached today.

[2] Peter was talking to the Believers in his day, as Christ's Disciples (Peter's contemporaries) understood well that their Lord and Master would return to them in their lifetime. This verse does not apply to those of us who are living today, as the Holy Spirit's presence never diminishes Himself throughout all generations from one age to the next, forevermore! See Mat.16:27; 24:34; Lk 21:22, 32; Jn 21:22; Acts 17:31; 24:15; 1 Cor. 7:29, 31; 10:11; Eph. 1:21; 1 Thess. 5:23; 2 Thess. 1:6-7; 5:23; 1 Tim. 4:8; 6:14, 19; James 5:7; 1 Peter 4:7, 17; 5:1; 1 Jn 2:8, 17-18; Rev. 1:1-3; 3:10-11; 22:6-7, 10, 12, 20. The Holy Spirit was withdrawn in AD 70 from all those whom God destroyed in the then of there – not "we" today!

[3] New Covenant Of Sovereign Grace replaced the Old Covenant of works and rituals. See Heb. 12:22-29.

[4] Peter is talking to the Believers of his day, not to us more than 2,000 years later!!

Hebrew Metaphoric Apocalyptic Language

Heavens: sun, stars, moon = Religious or political authorities (Genesis 37:9-10).

Earth: mountains, hills, valleys, waters = The place, person, nation involved in the prophecy.

Old Testament: Judgment upon Babylon (Isaiah 13); Idumea (Isaiah 34:4); Pharaoh of Egypt (Ezekiel 32:7-8); God's Enemies (Joel 2:10; 3:15-16); and David's Deliverance (2 Samuel 22:1-18).

New Testament: Roman Army used by God to administer judgment upon Jerusalem which was symbolically called Babylon (Revelation 17:5; 18:1-24) beginning in AD 66 and consummating in AD 70 (Matthew 24:29).

Second Meaning of Heavens/Earth = World/Age of Judaism Heavens: Divine Laws, Statues, Ordinances. **Earth**: Jerusalem, Temple, Canaan (land).

Old Testament: The world/age of Judaism established by God Himself (Jeremiah 18:9; Isaiah 51:15-16; Leviticus 26:18-19; Isaiah 1:1-2). Then, according to His Timetable, consummated the Old Covenant of laws into the New Covenant (Haggai 2:6-7; Isaiah 13:13).

New Testament: Jesus pointed forward to the end of the Jewish Age when He said: "Heaven and earth [Old Covenant: Administration] shall pass away, but my words shall not pass away" (Matthew 24:35). See 1 Corinthians 7:31; Hebrews 1:10-12; 8:13; Ephesians 2:14-15.

Coming In Clouds = In the Old Testament God "came down" many times – but not physically.

Old Testament: Tower of Babel (Genesis 11:5-6). **Q.** Was God actually seen when He "came down" to confound their language and scatter them? David's Deliverance (Psalm 18:7-16).

New Testament: The Hebrew Metaphoric Apocalyptic Language follows the same pattern in the New Testament. Christ fulfilled His promise to come down with clouds in deliverance and judgment (Acts 1:11; Luke 17:20; Revelation 14:14-16).

Elements Melt With Fervent Heat = *Elements* means ordinances [Old Covenant] which came to an end when Jerusalem was destroyed in AD 70.

Old Testament: Judgments of God were prophesied in Joel 2:10, 30-31.

New Testament: 2 Peter 3:10 is a description of the Old Covenant passing away, in preparation for God's New Covenant. See Galatians 4:3-10; Colossians 2:8, 20-22; Hebrews 5:12-14; 9:1.

New Heaven/New Earth = New Covenant Of Sovereign Grace written within each Born-Anew Believer.

Old Testament: Promise of New Covenant (Jeremiah 31:33; Isaiah 65:17-18).

New Testament: New Covenant fulfilled (Hebrews 10:15-18; Revelation 21:1).

World = People of the nation involved in the prophecy.

Old Testament: Isaiah 13:11.

New Testament: Revelation 3:10.

Day Of The Lord = Destruction of a nation by the power of God working through human armies.

Old Testament: Isaiah 13:6, 9; Ezekiel 13:5; 30:2-4; Joel 1:15; 2:1-2; 11; Amos 5:18; Obadiah 15; Zephaniah 1:7, 14.

New Testament: Acts 2:20; 1 Corinthians 1:8; 1 Thessalonians 5:2; 2 Thessalonians 2:2-12; 2 Peter 3:10-12; Revelation 6:17; 16:14-15.

Trumpet = Consolidation of God's people.

Old Testament: Isaiah 27:13.

New Testament: Matthew 24:31; 1 Corinthians 15:52; 1 Thessalonians 4:16.

Sun/Moon Darkened Or Turned To Blood = The darkness of a nation's distress, sorrow, and desolation.

Old Testament: Isaiah 13:9-11; 5:30; Ezekiel 30:18; 32:7-8; Amos 8:9; Zephaniah 1:14-15.

New Testament: Matthew 24:29; Acts 2:20; Revelation 6:12.

Shaking, Trembling, Or Earthquake = Power of God manifested in attacking human armies.

Old Testament: Jeremiah 51:29; Ezekiel 38:19-20.

New Testament: Revelation 16:18.

Sea Or Waters = A multitude or a nation of people.

Old Testament: Isaiah 5:30; 8:7; 18:2; Jeremiah 51:52.

New Testament: Revelation 4:6; 8:8; 21:1.

Harlot, Whore, Or Prostitute = A nation's unfaithfulness or apostasy to God.

Old Testament: Isaiah 1:21; Ezekiel 16:14-15; Hosea 1:2.

New Testament: Revelation 17:1-5; 18:3, 9; 19:2.

Babylon = A evil nation.

Old Testament: Isaiah 21:9.

New Testament: Revelation 14:8.

Eagle = Swift judgment and consequence through earthly armies.

Old Testament: Jeremiah 48:40; 49:22; Hosea 8:1; Habakkuk 1:8.

New Testament: Matthew 24:28; Revelation 4:7.

Carcase = A nation that is spiritually dead and militarily defeated.
Old Testament: Isa. 5:25; 14:19.
New Testament: Matt. 24:28.

Smoke = Desolation or destruction.
Old Testament: Isaiah 34:10; 14:31.
New Testament: Revelation 9:2; 14:11; 15:8; 18:9.

"Mountains, Cover Us" "Hills, Fall On Us" = Desperation for protection from destruction.
Old Testament: Hosea 10:8.
New Testament: Luke 23:30; Revelation 6:15-17.

Fire = The Power of the Word of God.
Old Testament: Jeremiah 23:29; Ezekiel 10:2; Zephaniah 1:18; 3:8; Zechariah 2:4-5.
New Testament: Hebrews 12:29; Revelation 8:5; 14:9-10.

Mountain = An earthly nation opposed to God.
Old Testament: Jeremiah 51:25; Micah 1:3-5.
New Testament: Revelation 6:14; 8:8; 16:20.

Pit Or Abyss = The destruction of nations by violence.
Old Testament: Ezekiel 26:20; 31:14-16; 32:18-20.
New Testament: Revelation 9:1-2.

Locust = Invading and attacking armies.
Old Testament: Joel 1:4-6; 2:4-5.
New Testament: Revelation 9:3-10.

Wormwood = Bitter effects of bad judgments.
Old Testament: Amos 5:7.
New Testament: Revelation 8:10-11.

Endtime Message Given To Daniel approx 600 BC - But Sealed - Danel 12:9-13 ←— 600 yrs —→ **Same Message Given To John The Revelator But Unsealed & Consummated in AD 70! Rev. 1:1, 3, 7 Rev. 22:10, 12, 20** ←——————————————→ **Not 2000+ Years And Holding!**

-42-

Four Living Creatures = Attributes of God.
Old Testament: Ezekiel 1:5-10.
New Testament: Revelation 4:6-7.

Cloud = Power in the spiritual realm/state.
Old Testament: Isaiah 19:1; Ezekiel 1:4.
New Testament: Matthew 24:30; Revelation 1:7.

Voice Like A Noise Of Many Waters - Powerful Words of God.
Old Testament: Ezekiel 43:2.
New Testament: Revelation 1:15.

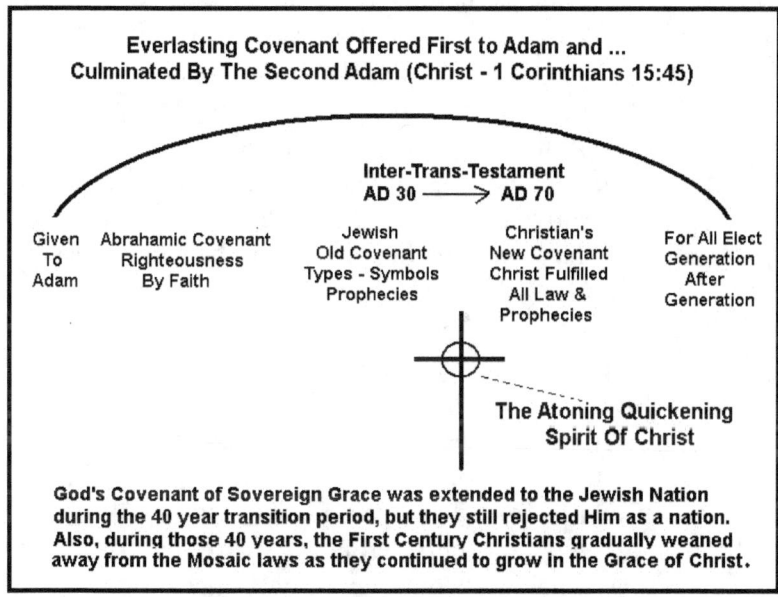

**Everlasting Covenant Offered First to Adam and ...
Culminated By The Second Adam (Christ - 1 Corinthians 15:45)**

**Inter-Trans-Testament
AD 30 ———> AD 70**

| Given To Adam | Abrahamic Covenant Righteousness By Faith | Jewish Old Covenant Types - Symbols Prophecies | Christian's New Covenant Christ Fulfilled All Law & Prophecies | For All Elect Generation After Generation |

The Atoning Quickening Spirit Of Christ

God's Covenant of Sovereign Grace was extended to the Jewish Nation during the 40 year transition period, but they still rejected Him as a nation. Also, during those 40 years, the First Century Christians gradually weaned away from the Mosaic laws as they continued to grow in the Grace of Christ.

Eating Of Scroll With Writing On Both Sides = The disclosure by God and reception by humans of specific knowledge.
Old Testament: Ezekiel 2:8-3:3.
New Testament: Revelation 5:1; 10:9-10

Mark Or Seal In Foreheads = Indication of righteousness or unrighteousness.
Old Testament: Ezekiel 9:3-6.
New Testament: Revelation 7:3; 9:4; 13:16-17.

Becoming Godly Kin
L. Phillip Schmidt

We've traveled paths you've perhaps known or been shown,
but not yet to have walked;
Learned lessons of Old Testament types and shadows, and
many more of fully-graced New!
And now this Wisdom-Strength of our Spiritual True Lives
which was once Titanically balked;
We're providing as Shareholders ... students ever learning
higher, with such – just like as you!
Kindness spread like sunshine's extensive rays among the
backed-up frayed and annoyed,
Embrace with graced-favor those who have made their
choices so sad ... and others so bad.
Respect their innate dignity, but moreso Godly manifestations
to them of those needing real joy;
And leave them with a taste of being once more glad, when
entwined in what seemed ironclad.
Forgive those who might willingly, unknowingly or
conversely belied themselves to subvertingly hurt you.
Though you may have your person to have a prideful stride –
pray Almighty God in all that betides.
Listen closely to more than some of others' viewpoints, even
though sometimes they seem askew.
Attempt to see one of many sides; because of plentiful
promises from the Divine's Unlimited Skies!
Tread softly when sortingly perplexed, misfitting, frustrated,
limited, tested, or upsettingly angry.
Attempt not to take illusioned or delusional vain offenses as
thoughts sitting on the highest fence.
Invoke still and yet your undiluted goodly-sense the best of
your sides the dynamite of good humor.
Laughter's power grants the highest release for your greatest
good, for its really implosively immense!
Express how, why and whereas you are or may be feeling a
temporary blight – or faithful plight to fight.
Believing them, is your own way to fold or uphold what
you've been told in – The Bible's – Centerfold [1].

Don't shy away from what – to others – seem imploringly half-sensed, misunderstood, or down-out not right.
Be courageous and never take arrogance to abstractedly mean being bold towards another's worthless scold!!
Keep hope in the righted corner of the safest uppermost part of your knowledgeable compassioned heart.
It will aid and assist you when and where, in and out, in mountains high, and valleys low day after day.
So, look to hope often, especially needful in trouble, woe and when stress or over-stress has a part.
Because as you keep it very near, you'll become more next-of-kin to God and eventually find a way!
Remember God first, spouse second, family third, then community and others knitting together in unity;
Of which you're considered included somehow and somewhat within and throughout a precious part –
Agape Love in its truest sense, and let other loss-losing-loves and the likes unjustly sound of impunity;
Giving freely of yourself in Jesus, all He has extended and purposed through your individual heart!
This world is far troubling and amiss of being any how's, where's, what's, or why's of being perfect,
To wit, there's conflicts, vice, wars, misapprehension, hard hearts, falsehood, and strife most everywhere;
But God's Favor through you can compassionately make the miraculous come to be circumspectly erect,
Simply by God's ordained complexity of Living In The Fullness Of His Life of too rich to compare!
And now, we're very comprisedly blessed beyond any comprehension or joyous measure to gracefully know;
The Beautiful Holy Works Of Righteousness The Living Christ will do in, for, by, through, and with you; anywhere you go!
Not fainting others; you will spiritually taste, hear, see, touch, and smell the Divine through one's mirroring glow,
Knowing The Triune, The Angels and we as believing in you to becoming next-of-kin through and through!

---

[1]The Bible's Centerfold is Psalm 119 cf. Romans 11:33

Our Faith Or His Faithfulness

L. Phillip Schmidt

It's not our feelings towards trusting so much,
As our faith corresponding to His Graceful Touch.

And when nothing changes, bends or mends as we thought;
He is ever teaching His Faithfulness to us whom He bought!

Look up where Christ rose to the Heavenly Eternal Height,
For He will bring you up from each and every earthly plight.

Deliver you He will as you yield all cares and sorrows,
The Victor and Friend in all of your days and tomorrows!

The Kingdom Of God Is Within You

Esther Grace Schmidt

It is such a glorious thought to know
What Jesus said so long ago,
"The Kingdom of God IS within you!"

This Kingdom does not come by outward show,
But peacefully abides within our inner soul,
"The Kingdom of God IS within you!"

How can this Kingdom be in a building made with hands?
As Scripture clearly tells us of His Almighty Sovereign Plans,
"The Kingdom of God IS within you."

This Kingdom of God is still being built
Jesus paid the penalty to free a repentant sinner of all guilt,
"The Kingdom of God IS within you."

Called Of God – And Chosen To Tell It As He Is!
L. Phillip Schmidt

I have studied the Bible after men's thoughts
And came back to kindergarten!

I have studied the Bible philosophically
And came back to kindergarten!

I have studied the Bible by many commentaries
And came back to kindergarten!

I have studied the Bible of dogmas theological
machinery
And came back to kindergarten!

I have studied the Bible in the *Science of Nature*
And came back to kindergarten!

I have studied the Bible in so many other ways;
But I found out – to stay in – The Kinder-Garden!

A nod for each one of you too, to being the "Very Kin
Of God,"
And a "*Tree Of Righteousness*" in His Kinder-Garden!

Reflections

- Believers can be assured God can and will still manifest His Supernatural Power in behalf of His People.

- Have you ever considered that most animals are true to themselves and to God than people are true to themselves and to God?

- The more Godly Love one has, the greater caring responsibility of accountabilities rests in time, place and circumstantial situational ethics, for fairness in physical, mental, spiritual, and soul (will/mind/emotions) matters.

- In being Salvationed by God's Favor ... within Merciful Compassion ... and throughout His Amazing Grace, it behooves the most intelligent minds of the manifold turnings God successfully guides each adopted child through and for kaleidoscopic meaningfulness(es) beings the sum total of such is greater than the whole of all the parts of theological and ethical manifestations.

- All things needful will come to those who wait patiently in their darkness of the stillness of the quietness of their souls; because things are not the most important things; and further, because serving others in the heartfelt capacity God endows each one with, will find the solaced value advantaging others growth, enlargement, enlightenment, and advancement; and the furthering of peace with God; thus they will be less and less disturbed by the invasions of the profane. See Matthew 26:53 (explanation: 12 legions is 80,000 angels!).

- By allowing God's Spirit of Love to guide us unconditionally; and understanding that He Who writes the Rule of The Spirit determines the results and the outcome because HE IS the Law of the Spirit forever and giving every Believer a Peace that truly passes all understanding!

- We trust and rely on the Revelation, Authority, and Function; that which effectively causes God the Father's Revelation of Himself through giving His Son all the Authoritative Judgment concerning Salvationing through the alongside Function of the Holy Spirit to accomplish and culminate every detail in order to pass from the valley of the physical temporary life onto the Divine Life Everlasting in the Spiritual Eternal Realm forever and ever!

- If one conflicts with God's Creation of Nature, She will win every time! She was here before anyone came on the scene, and will be here when he/she/we/us are no longer!
- Everything in nature promotes itself to glorifying God; which teaches us to look up and have a more Abundant Life through God's Miracle Working Power.
- Just imagine how God led the First Century Believers and blessed them. To most people's minds, God was finished with His Miracle Power, but all of history agrees that there is one Miracle that stands out above all others in that God Transforms lives to do His Good Pleasure!
- The question comes up, "Does God's Supernatural Power still surpass the natural? Yes. There is one thing which can always be counted on. He still transforms a sinner's natural tendencies to evil into a Spiritual Nature having a firm desire to Praise, Honor and Glorify Him in all he/she thinks, says and does!
- Believer, keep in the Way, Truth, and Life of Christ by daily studying His Word in [Its] height, depth, width, and breadth; and by so doing please your Saviour, Lord and Master; for He Wills you be kept from the darknesses of susceptible counterings of the cults, skeptics, other religions, philosophies, universalism, Christadelphianism, and Annihilationism which become serious problems that have compromised with the hedonistic and materialistic cultures around and about you.
- Sinners all have a future of promise in Christ! Saints all have had a past of sorrow and regret with the antichrist!
- Focus upon the all, full, and whole of what God has done for you; and less and less of all the fragmentations others attempt to misalign you with!!
- Which is greater: man walking on the moon, OR God walking on the earth?

A Personal Invitation
Quoted From The Contemporary Bible THE MESSAGE

Are you tired? Worn out? Burned out on religion? *Come to me.* Get away with me *and you'll recover your life.* I'll show you how to take a real rest. Walk with me and work with me – watch how I do it. *Learn the unforced rhythms of grace.* I won't lay anything heavy or ill-fitting on you. *Keep company with me and you'll learn to live freely and lightly.*" Matthew 11:28-30 [lps].

"You're blessed when you're at the end of your rope. With less of you there is more of God and his rule. You're blessed when you feel you've lost what is most dear to you. Only then can you be embraced by the One most dear to you.

"You're blessed when you're content with just who you are – no more, no less. That's the moment you find yourselves proud owners of everything that can't be bought.

"You're blessed when you've worked up a good appetite for God. He's food and drink in the best meal you'll ever eat.

"You're blessed when you care. At the moment of being 'care-full,' you find yourselves cared for.

"You're blessed when you get your inside world – your mind and heart – put right. Then you can see God in the outside world.

"You're blessed when you can show people how to cooperate instead of compete or fight. That's when you discover who you really are, and your place in God's family.

"You're blessed when your commitment to God provokes persecution [trouble]. The persecution drives you even deeper into God's kingdom.

"Not only that – count yourselves blessed every time people put you down or throw you out or speak lies about you to discredit me. What it means is that the truth is too close for comfort and they are uncomfortable. You can be glad when that happens – give a cheer, even! – for though they don't like it, I do! And all heaven applauds. And know that you are in good company. My prophets and witnesses have always gotten into this kind of trouble." Matthew 5:3-12 [lps].

Subscribe To More Spiritually Recondite Books
Of Biblical Excellence!

- *Confronting The Altruistic Values Of Christ To The Seventh-day Adventist Church* by L. Phillip Schmidt. A much needed exposé written by a former member of their cultic organization of his personal experience in recovering from their delusive power strugglings and falsified teachings. He has a great concern for those who are still in similar pseudo and quasi bondages, and desires to warn those who are unaware of these false gospel dangers. Order from: Amazon.com

- *A Love Letter: From Your Most High God ...To You, My Spirit Born Child* by Esther Grace Schmidt and L. Phillip Schmidt. Order from: Amazon.com

- *Christianity's Great Dilemma – Is Jesus Coming Again or Is He Not?* by Glenn L. Hill. Order from: Amazon.com

- *The Fulfilled Covenant Bible,*© Michael Day. Bible and commentary on each book. Order from: Amazon.com

- *Beyond The Veil Of Moses*, by Brian Martin. Order from: Preterist.org

- *The Complete Works Of Josephus*, translated by William Whiston; commentary by Paul L. Maier. Order from: Preterist.org

- *Anno Domini LXX: In the year of our Lord 70,* a novel by George Dannenberg. Order from: Amazon.com

- *What Happened In A.D. 70?* by Edward E. Stevens. Order from: Preterist.org

- *Results Of Fulfilled Prophecy* by Jessie E. Mills, Jr. Order from: Preterist.org

- *Revelation Survey and Research,* by Jessie E. Mills, Jr. Order from: Preterist.org

- *Unique Revisitations Of God's Merciful Grace* by L. Phillip Schmidt and Esther Schmidt[1]. Order from: Amazon.com

- *Eternal Riches Of God's Glory For Every Disciple of*

Christ's Kingdom: A Guide For Individual Or Group Study of Attributes Given The Moment One Is Spiritually Born-Anew by L. Phillip Schmidt and Esther Schmidt[1]. Order from: Amazon.com

- *The Everlasting Faithfulness And Unstoppable Promises Of God* by L. Phillip Schmidt and Esther Schmidt[1]. Order from: Amazon.com
- *Christ's Spiritual Blessings To You* by L. Phillip Schmidt and Esther Schmidt[1]. Order from: Amazon.com
- *Trusting Jesus As Our Best Friend* by Esther Schmidt[1] and L. Phillip Schmidt. A book for boys and girls emphasizing the gracious love Jesus has for them. Order from: Amazon.com
- *Essential Diversified Desk Notes Of Repose For The Spirit: We Live To Learn Until We Learn To Live!* by L. Phillip Schmidt and Esther Grace Schmidt. Order from: Amazon.com
- *James Fulfilled: From Persecuted To Perfected* by T. Everett Denton. Order from: Amazon.com.
- *Pertinent Parousia Passages: Second-Coming Scripture Studies* by T. Everett Denton. Order from: Amazon.com.
- *Rich Christians In An Age Of Hunger: Moving From Affluence To Generosity* by Ronald J. Sider. Order from: Amazon.com
- *The Blessedness of Spiritual Living: Revealing The Holy Spirit's Magnanimity Through Ministry* by Esther Grace Schmidt and L. Phillip Schmidt. Order from; Amazon.com.
- *Spiritual Guidance Through Psalms And Proverbs* by L Phillip Schmidt and Esther Grace Schmidt. Order from: Amazon.com.
- *Churchism In The Church Age* by Bill Young. Order from: Amazon.com

---

[1]The name of Esther Schmidt was changed to Esther Grace Schmidt after she co-authored this book.

Authors' Note. It has been our pleasure to bring our literary inclinations to benefit your Newness in Christ, Spiritual Growth, Soul Enlargements, and Physical Endowments through this brief study of Nature and the many Spiritual Lessons we learn from all the things Our Creator has made for our pleasure and enjoyment. Be free to contact us as we would be most pleased to learn what the Lord has done and/or is still doing for you! The Prophet Isaiah declared: "I will recount the loving-kindnesses of the Lord and the praiseworthy deeds of the Lord, according to all that the Lord has bestowed on us." Isaiah 63:7a (Amp.). As maturing Christians, all of us are beholding into the finishing within God's furnishing throughout God's Holiness from day to day! You may address your personal testimony, comments, questions, and/or suggestions to:

highcalling8@twc.com
Also Visit Our Website:
www.CovenantSovereignGrace.com

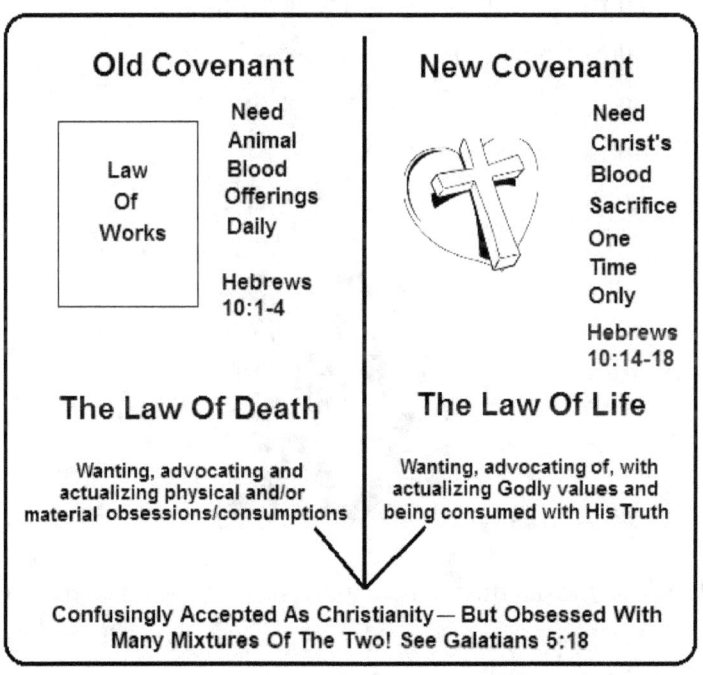

Authors' Disclaimer. The usage and/or provision of any or all of the contents within this book is the full and total responsibility of the recipient for each individual's provenances and/or acknowledgments, and none of the authors' pari passu (without preference or priority). 1 Corinthians 15:34; Galatians 6:5.

The Valley Of Vision

from Valley of Vision, a collection of Puritan Prayers

Lord, high and holy, meek and lowly, Thou hast brought me to the valley of vision, where I live in the depths but see Thee in the heights; hemmed by mountains of sin I behold Thy Glory. Let me learn by paradox ...

That the way down is the way up,

That to be low is to be high,

That the broken heart is the healed heart,

That the contrite spirit is the rejoicing spirit,

That the repenting soul is the victorious soul,

That to have nothing is to possess all,

That to bear the cross is to wear the crown,

That to give is to receive,

That the valley is the place of vision.

Lord, in the daytime stars can be seen from the deepest wells, and the deeper the wells the brighter Thy stars shine. Let me find Thy Light in my darkness ...

Thy life in my death,

Thy joy in my sorrow,

Thy grace in my poverty

Thy glory in my valley.